HARD NUTS
OF HISTORY

Play the
Game

TRACEY TURNER
ILLUSTRATED BY JAMIE LENMAN

A & C BLACK
AN IMPRINT OF BLOOMSBURY
LONDON   NEW DELHI   NEW YORK   SYDNEY

First published 2015 by

A & C Black, an imprint of Bloomsbury Publishing Plc

50 Bedford Square, London WC1B 3DP

www.bloomsbury.com

Bloomsbury is a registered trademark of Bloomsbury Publishing Plc

ISBN 978-1-4729-1097-4

A CIP catalogue for this book is available from the British Library.

Printed in China by Leo Paper Products, Heshan, Guangdong

1 3 5 7 9 10 8 6 4 2

INTRODUCTION

Prepare to do battle with some of the hardest nuts of history . . .

FIND OUT . . .

• **Who was the bravest ancient Greek warrior?**

• **Which was the most ruthless Roman general?**

• **Who was the most cunning warrior of all?**

• **Which intrepid explorer had the best survival skills?**

• **Who was the hardest nut of myths and legends?**

Some of these hard nuts won battles, some conquered empires, and some started revolutions. They ruled millions of subjects, crossed uncharted territory, killed terrifying monsters and all of them were as hard as nails. Each tough nut character has a rating for cunning, courage, survival skills and ruthlessness. They are also surrounded by a different colour to indicate where they come from or what they did:

Blue: Ancient Greece   Purple: Wars and Battles

Yellow: Ancient Rome   Dark Green: Travellers and Explorers

Green: Ancient Egypt   Dark Red: Kings and Queens

Red: Warriors   Turquoise: Myths and Legends

Play the game and take on your friends and family to find out if Cleopatra was more cunning than Julius Caesar, or whether Wellington had better survival skills than Napoleon.

Turn the page for instructions on how to play.

BATTLE OF THE HARD NUTS

HOW TO PLAY

This game can be played by two or more players. Cut out the cards and shuffle and deal an equal number to each player. The player who starts must choose a category from his or her topmost card. They can choose from either the *Hardometer* scores or the overall *Hard Nut Rating*.

The other players must then give the score for the same category from their top card. The player with the highest score wins the opposing player's top card/s. In the event of a draw, the cards are placed in the centre and a new category is selected from the next card by the same person.

CUNNING: 6
COURAGE: 7
SURVIVAL SKILLS: 7
RUTHLESSNESS: 7

The winner of that round gets all of the cards in the centre as well as the top card from each player.

The winner is the player who obtains the whole pack. Good luck, and may the hardest nut win!

BUCEPHALIA
ALEXANDRIA
ALEXANDRIA
ALEXANDRIA
ALEXANDRIA
ALEXANDRIA
ALEXANDRIA
ALEXANDRIA
ALEXANDRIA
ALEXANDRIA
ALEXANDRIA
ALEXANDRIA
ALEXANDRIA
ALEXANDRIA

HARDOMETER

CUNNING: 8
COURAGE: 8
SURVIVAL SKILLS: 8
RUTHLESSNESS: 9

HARD NUT
RATING: 8.3

ALEXANDER THE GREAT

JULIUS CAESAR

HARD NUT
RATING: 8.3

HARDOMETER

CUNNING: 8
COURAGE: 9
SURVIVAL SKILLS: 7
RUTHLESSNESS: 9

CLEOPATRA

HARD NUT
RATING: 7.8

HARDOMETER

CUNNING: 8
COURAGE: 8
SURVIVAL SKILLS: 7
RUTHLESSNESS: 8

BABUR

HARD NUT
RATING: 8.5

HARDOMETER

CUNNING: 9
COURAGE: 8
SURVIVAL SKILLS: 9
RUTHLESSNESS: 8

HARD NUTS
of HISTORY

A & C BLACK
AN IMPRINT OF BLOOMSBURY
LONDON NEW DELHI NEW YORK SYDNEY

HARD NUTS
of HISTORY

A & C BLACK
AN IMPRINT OF BLOOMSBURY
LONDON NEW DELHI NEW YORK SYDNEY

HARD NUTS
of HISTORY

A & C BLACK
AN IMPRINT OF BLOOMSBURY
LONDON NEW DELHI NEW YORK SYDNEY

HARD NUTS
of HISTORY

A & C BLACK
AN IMPRINT OF BLOOMSBURY
LONDON NEW DELHI NEW YORK SYDNEY

HARD NUT
RATING: 6.8

HARDOMETER

CUNNING: 6
COURAGE: 7
SURVIVAL SKILLS: 7
RUTHLESSNESS: 7

CHRISTOPHER COLUMBUS

HERACLES

HARD NUT
RATING: 10

HARDOMETER

CUNNING: 10
COURAGE: 10
SURVIVAL SKILLS: 10
RUTHLESSNESS: 10

FERDINAND AND ISABELLA

HARDOMETER

CUNNING: 7
COURAGE: 6
SURVIVAL SKILLS: 9
RUTHLESSNESS: 9

HARD NUT
RATING: 7.8

THE DUKE OF WELLINGTON

HARD NUT
RATING: 8.3

HARDOMETER

CUNNING: 9
COURAGE: 8
SURVIVAL SKILLS: 8
RUTHLESSNESS: 8

HARD NUTS OF HISTORY

A & C BLACK
AN IMPRINT OF BLOOMSBURY

LONDON   NEW DELHI   NEW YORK   SYDNEY

HARD NUTS OF HISTORY

A & C BLACK
AN IMPRINT OF BLOOMSBURY

LONDON   NEW DELHI   NEW YORK   SYDNEY

HARD NUTS OF HISTORY

A & C BLACK
AN IMPRINT OF BLOOMSBURY

LONDON   NEW DELHI   NEW YORK   SYDNEY

HARD NUTS OF HISTORY

A & C BLACK
AN IMPRINT OF BLOOMSBURY

LONDON   NEW DELHI   NEW YORK   SYDNEY

SIMÓN BOLÍVAR

HARD NUT
RATING: 7.3

HARDOMETER

CUNNING: 7
COURAGE: 8
SURVIVAL SKILLS: 6
RUTHLESSNESS: 8

HARALD HARDRADA

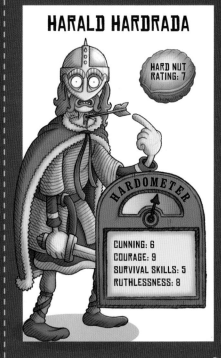

HARD NUT
RATING: 7

HARDOMETER

CUNNING: 6
COURAGE: 9
SURVIVAL SKILLS: 5
RUTHLESSNESS: 8

AUGUSTUS CAESAR

FIRST
CITIZEN

HARD NUT
RATING: 9

HARDOMETER

CUNNING: 9
COURAGE: 9
SURVIVAL SKILLS: 9
RUTHLESSNESS: 9

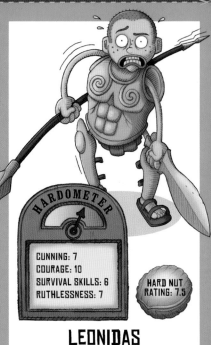

HARDOMETER

CUNNING: 7
COURAGE: 10
SURVIVAL SKILLS: 6
RUTHLESSNESS: 7

HARD NUT
RATING: 7.5

LEONIDAS

HARD NUTS of HISTORY

A & C BLACK
AN IMPRINT OF BLOOMSBURY
LONDON   NEW DELHI   NEW YORK   SYDNEY

HARD NUTS of HISTORY

A & C BLACK
AN IMPRINT OF BLOOMSBURY
LONDON   NEW DELHI   NEW YORK   SYDNEY

HARD NUTS of HISTORY

A & C BLACK
AN IMPRINT OF BLOOMSBURY
LONDON   NEW DELHI   NEW YORK   SYDNEY

HARD NUTS of HISTORY

A & C BLACK
AN IMPRINT OF BLOOMSBURY
LONDON   NEW DELHI   NEW YORK   SYDNEY

HARD NUT RATING: 8.5

HARDOMETER

CUNNING: 8
COURAGE: 8
SURVIVAL SKILLS: 9
RUTHLESSNESS: 9

GENGHIS KHAN

KING PIYE

HARDOMETER

CUNNING: 9
COURAGE: 9
SURVIVAL SKILLS: 9
RUTHLESSNESS: 9

HARD NUT RATING: 9

BEOWULF

HARD NUT RATING: 9.8

HARDOMETER

CUNNING: 10
COURAGE: 10
SURVIVAL SKILLS: 9
RUTHLESSNESS: 10

HARD NUT RATING: 7

HARDOMETER

CUNNING: 7
COURAGE: 10
SURVIVAL SKILLS: 6
RUTHLESSNESS: 5

AMELIA EARHART

HARD NUTS
of HISTORY

A & C BLACK
AN IMPRINT OF BLOOMSBURY
LONDON   NEW DELHI   NEW YORK   SYDNEY

HARD NUTS
of HISTORY

A & C BLACK
AN IMPRINT OF BLOOMSBURY
LONDON   NEW DELHI   NEW YORK   SYDNEY

HARD NUTS
of HISTORY

A & C BLACK
AN IMPRINT OF BLOOMSBURY
LONDON   NEW DELHI   NEW YORK   SYDNEY

HARD NUTS
of HISTORY

A & C BLACK
AN IMPRINT OF BLOOMSBURY
LONDON   NEW DELHI   NEW YORK   SYDNEY

HARD NUT RATING: 5

HARDOMETER

CUNNING: 5
COURAGE: 10
SURVIVAL SKILLS: 5
RUTHLESSNESS: 0

SOCRATES

HANNIBAL

HARD NUT RATING: 7.8

HARDOMETER

CUNNING: 8
COURAGE: 9
SURVIVAL SKILLS: 8
RUTHLESSNESS: 6

TUTANKHAMUN

HARD NUT RATING: 6.3

HARDOMETER

CUNNING: 6
COURAGE: 8
SURVIVAL SKILLS: 4
RUTHLESSNESS: 7

GERONIMO

HARD NUT RATING: 8.3

HARDOMETER

CUNNING: 7
COURAGE: 9
SURVIVAL SKILLS: 8
RUTHLESSNESS: 9

HARD NUTS
OF HISTORY

A & C BLACK
AN IMPRINT OF BLOOMSBURY
LONDON   NEW DELHI   NEW YORK   SYDNEY

HARD NUTS
OF HISTORY

A & C BLACK
AN IMPRINT OF BLOOMSBURY
LONDON   NEW DELHI   NEW YORK   SYDNEY

HARD NUTS
OF HISTORY

A & C BLACK
AN IMPRINT OF BLOOMSBURY
LONDON   NEW DELHI   NEW YORK   SYDNEY

HARD NUTS
OF HISTORY

A & C BLACK
AN IMPRINT OF BLOOMSBURY
LONDON   NEW DELHI   NEW YORK   SYDNEY

HARD NUT
RATING: 8.3

HARDOMETER

CUNNING: 8
COURAGE: 9
SURVIVAL SKILLS: 8
RUTHLESSNESS: 8

CAPTAIN COOK

HUA MULAN

HARD NUT
RATING: 9

HARDOMETER

CUNNING: 10
COURAGE: 9
SURVIVAL SKILLS: 9
RUTHLESSNESS: 8

NZINGA
MBANDE

HARD NUT
RATING: 7.5

HARDOMETER

CUNNING: 8
COURAGE: 8
SURVIVAL SKILLS: 9
RUTHLESSNESS: 5

LEON
TROTSKY

HARD NUT
RATING: 8

HARDOMETER

CUNNING: 9
COURAGE: 9
SURVIVAL SKILLS: 7
RUTHLESSNESS: 7

HARD NUTS
of HISTORY

A & C BLACK
AN IMPRINT OF BLOOMSBURY
LONDON   NEW DELHI   NEW YORK   SYDNEY

HARD NUTS
of HISTORY

A & C BLACK
AN IMPRINT OF BLOOMSBURY
LONDON   NEW DELHI   NEW YORK   SYDNEY

HARD NUTS
of HISTORY

A & C BLACK
AN IMPRINT OF BLOOMSBURY
LONDON   NEW DELHI   NEW YORK   SYDNEY

HARD NUTS
of HISTORY

A & C BLACK
AN IMPRINT OF BLOOMSBURY
LONDON   NEW DELHI   NEW YORK   SYDNEY

GENERAL CUSTER

HARD NUT
RATING: 8.3

CUNNING: 7
COURAGE: 9
SURVIVAL SKILLS: 8
RUTHLESSNESS: 9

HENRY VIII

HARD NUT
RATING: 7.3

CUNNING: 8
COURAGE: 6
SURVIVAL SKILLS: 5
RUTHLESSNESS: 10

SPARTACUS

CUNNING: 9
COURAGE: 9
SURVIVAL SKILLS: 7
RUTHLESSNESS: 7

HARD NUT
RATING: 8

HYPATIA

HARD NUT
RATING: 6.3

CUNNING: 5
COURAGE: 9
SURVIVAL SKILLS: 6
RUTHLESSNESS: 5

HARD NUTS of HISTORY

A & C BLACK
AN IMPRINT OF BLOOMSBURY
LONDON   NEW DELHI   NEW YORK   SYDNEY

HARD NUTS of HISTORY

A & C BLACK
AN IMPRINT OF BLOOMSBURY
LONDON   NEW DELHI   NEW YORK   SYDNEY

HARD NUTS of HISTORY

A & C BLACK
AN IMPRINT OF BLOOMSBURY
LONDON   NEW DELHI   NEW YORK   SYDNEY

HARD NUTS of HISTORY

A & C BLACK
AN IMPRINT OF BLOOMSBURY
LONDON   NEW DELHI   NEW YORK   SYDNEY

JOAN OF ARC

HARD NUT RATING: 7

HARDOMETER

CUNNING: 7
COURAGE: 9
SURVIVAL SKILLS: 5
RUTHLESSNESS: 7

QUEEN NEFERTITI

HARD NUT RATING: 7.3

HARDOMETER

CUNNING: 7
COURAGE: 7
SURVIVAL SKILLS: 6
RUTHLESSNESS: 9

CÚ CHULAINN

HARD NUT RATING: 8.3

HARDOMETER

CUNNING: 8
COURAGE: 9
SURVIVAL SKILLS: 7
RUTHLESSNESS: 9

HERNÁN CORTÉS

HARD NUT RATING: 8.8

HARDOMETER

CUNNING: 8
COURAGE: 9
SURVIVAL SKILLS: 8
RUTHLESSNESS: 10

HARD NUTS
of HISTORY

A & C BLACK
AN IMPRINT OF BLOOMSBURY
LONDON NEW DELHI NEW YORK SYDNEY

HARD NUTS
of HISTORY

A & C BLACK
AN IMPRINT OF BLOOMSBURY
LONDON NEW DELHI NEW YORK SYDNEY

HARD NUTS
of HISTORY

A & C BLACK
AN IMPRINT OF BLOOMSBURY
LONDON NEW DELHI NEW YORK SYDNEY

HARD NUTS
of HISTORY

A & C BLACK
AN IMPRINT OF BLOOMSBURY
LONDON NEW DELHI NEW YORK SYDNEY

ARCHIMEDES

HARD NUT RATING: 6.3

EUREKA!

HARDOMETER

CUNNING: 8
COURAGE: 8
SURVIVAL SKILLS: 5
RUTHLESSNESS: 4

EMPEROR NERO

HARD NUT RATING: 7.8

HARDOMETER

CUNNING: 7
COURAGE: 8
SURVIVAL SKILLS: 6
RUTHLESSNESS: 10

THUTMOSE III

HARD NUT RATING: 9

HARDOMETER

CUNNING: 9
COURAGE: 9
SURVIVAL SKILLS: 9
RUTHLESSNESS: 9

TOMYRIS

HARD NUT RATING: 9.3

HARDOMETER

CUNNING: 9
COURAGE: 9
SURVIVAL SKILLS: 10
RUTHLESSNESS: 9

HARD NUTS
of HISTORY

A & C BLACK
AN IMPRINT OF BLOOMSBURY
LONDON   NEW DELHI   NEW YORK   SYDNEY

HARD NUTS
of HISTORY

A & C BLACK
AN IMPRINT OF BLOOMSBURY
LONDON   NEW DELHI   NEW YORK   SYDNEY

HARD NUTS
of HISTORY

A & C BLACK
AN IMPRINT OF BLOOMSBURY
LONDON   NEW DELHI   NEW YORK   SYDNEY

HARD NUTS
of HISTORY

A & C BLACK
AN IMPRINT OF BLOOMSBURY
LONDON   NEW DELHI   NEW YORK   SYDNEY

VINLAND

HARD NUT RATING: 8.5

HARDOMETER

CUNNING: 8
COURAGE: 9
SURVIVAL SKILLS: 9
RUTHLESSNESS: 8

LEIF ERICSON

THOR

HARD NUT RATING: 9.3

HARDOMETER

CUNNING: 8
COURAGE: 10
SURVIVAL SKILLS: 9
RUTHLESSNESS: 10

KING KAMEHAMEHA I

HARD NUT RATING: 8

HARDOMETER

CUNNING: 8
COURAGE: 9
SURVIVAL SKILLS: 7
RUTHLESSNESS: 8

FLORA SANDES

HARD NUT RATING: 8

HARDOMETER

CUNNING: 8
COURAGE: 10
SURVIVAL SKILLS: 8
RUTHLESSNESS: 6

HARD NUTS
of HISTORY

A & C BLACK
AN IMPRINT OF BLOOMSBURY
LONDON   NEW DELHI   NEW YORK   SYDNEY

HARD NUTS
of HISTORY

A & C BLACK
AN IMPRINT OF BLOOMSBURY
LONDON   NEW DELHI   NEW YORK   SYDNEY

HARD NUTS
of HISTORY

A & C BLACK
AN IMPRINT OF BLOOMSBURY
LONDON   NEW DELHI   NEW YORK   SYDNEY

HARD NUTS
of HISTORY

A & C BLACK
AN IMPRINT OF BLOOMSBURY
LONDON   NEW DELHI   NEW YORK   SYDNEY

HARDOMETER

CUNNING: 10
COURAGE: 10
SURVIVAL SKILLS: 9
RUTHLESSNESS: 8

HARD NUT RATING: 9.3

DEBORAH SAMPSON

KING SHAKA

HARD NUT RATING: 8

HARDOMETER

CUNNING: 8
COURAGE: 7
SURVIVAL SKILLS: 7
RUTHLESSNESS: 10

AGRIPPINA

HARD NUT RATING: 8.8

HARDOMETER

CUNNING: 9
COURAGE: 9
SURVIVAL SKILLS: 8
RUTHLESSNESS: 9

DARIUS THE GREAT

HARD NUT RATING: 8.5

HARDOMETER

CUNNING: 9
COURAGE: 8
SURVIVAL SKILLS: 8
RUTHLESSNESS: 9

HARD NUTS
of HISTORY

A & C BLACK
AN IMPRINT OF BLOOMSBURY
LONDON NEW DELHI NEW YORK SYDNEY

HARD NUTS
of HISTORY

A & C BLACK
AN IMPRINT OF BLOOMSBURY
LONDON NEW DELHI NEW YORK SYDNEY

HARD NUTS
of HISTORY

A & C BLACK
AN IMPRINT OF BLOOMSBURY
LONDON NEW DELHI NEW YORK SYDNEY

HARD NUTS
of HISTORY

A & C BLACK
AN IMPRINT OF BLOOMSBURY
LONDON NEW DELHI NEW YORK SYDNEY

CHARLEMAGNE

HARD NUT RATING: 8

CUNNING: 8
COURAGE: 8
SURVIVAL SKILLS: 8
RUTHLESSNESS: 8

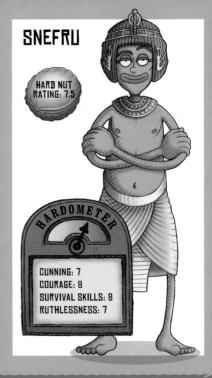

SNEFRU

HARD NUT RATING: 7.5

CUNNING: 7
COURAGE: 8
SURVIVAL SKILLS: 8
RUTHLESSNESS: 7

DURGA

HARD NUT RATING: 9

CUNNING: 9
COURAGE: 9
SURVIVAL SKILLS: 9
RUTHLESSNESS: 9

FERDINAND MAGELLAN

HARD NUT RATING: 8.3

CUNNING: 8
COURAGE: 9
SURVIVAL SKILLS: 6
RUTHLESSNESS: 10

HARD NUTS
of HISTORY

A & C BLACK
AN IMPRINT OF BLOOMSBURY
LONDON   NEW DELHI   NEW YORK   SYDNEY

HARD NUTS
of HISTORY

A & C BLACK
AN IMPRINT OF BLOOMSBURY
LONDON   NEW DELHI   NEW YORK   SYDNEY

HARD NUTS
of HISTORY

A & C BLACK
AN IMPRINT OF BLOOMSBURY
LONDON   NEW DELHI   NEW YORK   SYDNEY

HARD NUTS
of HISTORY

A & C BLACK
AN IMPRINT OF BLOOMSBURY
LONDON   NEW DELHI   NEW YORK   SYDNEY

PHEIDIPPIDES

HARDOMETER

CUNNING: 6
COURAGE: 9
SURVIVAL SKILLS: 6
RUTHLESSNESS: 5

HARD NUT
RATING: 6.5

HARD NUT
RATING: 8

HARDOMETER

CUNNING: 8
COURAGE: 9
SURVIVAL SKILLS: 7
RUTHLESSNESS: 8

MARK
ANTONY

HATSHEPSUT

HARD NUT
RATING: 8.8

HARDOMETER

CUNNING: 10
COURAGE: 8
SURVIVAL SKILLS: 9
RUTHLESSNESS: 8

TOMOE GOZEN

HARDOMETER

CUNNING: 7
COURAGE: 9
SURVIVAL SKILLS: 6
RUTHLESSNESS: 8

HARD NUT
RATING: 7.5

HARD NUTS
OF HISTORY

A & C BLACK
AN IMPRINT OF BLOOMSBURY
LONDON NEW DELHI NEW YORK SYDNEY

HARD NUTS
OF HISTORY

A & C BLACK
AN IMPRINT OF BLOOMSBURY
LONDON NEW DELHI NEW YORK SYDNEY

HARD NUTS
OF HISTORY

A & C BLACK
AN IMPRINT OF BLOOMSBURY
LONDON NEW DELHI NEW YORK SYDNEY

HARD NUTS
OF HISTORY

A & C BLACK
AN IMPRINT OF BLOOMSBURY
LONDON NEW DELHI NEW YORK SYDNEY

MARCO POLO

HARDOMETER

CUNNING: 8
COURAGE: 8
SURVIVAL SKILLS: 8
RUTHLESSNESS: 7

HARD NUT RATING: 7.8

MEDEA

HARD NUT RATING: 9.5

HARDOMETER

CUNNING: 10
COURAGE: 8
SURVIVAL SKILLS: 10
RUTHLESSNESS: 10

FREDERICK THE GREAT

HARD NUT RATING: 7.5

HARDOMETER

CUNNING: 7
COURAGE: 7
SURVIVAL SKILLS: 8
RUTHLESSNESS: 8

DAVY CROCKETT

HARD NUT RATING: 7.3

HARDOMETER

CUNNING: 7
COURAGE: 9
SURVIVAL SKILLS: 5
RUTHLESSNESS: 8

HARD NUTS
of HISTORY

A & C BLACK
AN IMPRINT OF BLOOMSBURY

LONDON   NEW DELHI   NEW YORK   SYDNEY

HARD NUTS
of HISTORY

A & C BLACK
AN IMPRINT OF BLOOMSBURY

LONDON   NEW DELHI   NEW YORK   SYDNEY

HARD NUTS
of HISTORY

A & C BLACK
AN IMPRINT OF BLOOMSBURY

LONDON   NEW DELHI   NEW YORK   SYDNEY

HARD NUTS
of HISTORY

A & C BLACK
AN IMPRINT OF BLOOMSBURY

LONDON   NEW DELHI   NEW YORK   SYDNEY

MARY SEACOLE

HARD NUT RATING: 8.3

HARDOMETER

CUNNING: 9
COURAGE: 10
SURVIVAL SKILLS: 9
RUTHLESSNESS: 5

MONTEZUMA II

HARD NUT RATING: 7.5

HARDOMETER

CUNNING: 7
COURAGE: 8
SURVIVAL SKILLS: 6
RUTHLESSNESS: 9

POMPEY THE GREAT

HARD NUT RATING: 8.8

HARDOMETER

CUNNING: 9
COURAGE: 9
SURVIVAL SKILLS: 8
RUTHLESSNESS: 9

XERXES THE GREAT

HARD NUT RATING: 7.5

HARDOMETER

CUNNING: 6
COURAGE: 7
SURVIVAL SKILLS: 7
RUTHLESSNESS: 10

HARD NUTS
of HISTORY

A & C BLACK
AN IMPRINT OF BLOOMSBURY
LONDON   NEW DELHI   NEW YORK   SYDNEY

HARD NUTS
of HISTORY

A & C BLACK
AN IMPRINT OF BLOOMSBURY
LONDON   NEW DELHI   NEW YORK   SYDNEY

HARD NUTS
of HISTORY

A & C BLACK
AN IMPRINT OF BLOOMSBURY
LONDON   NEW DELHI   NEW YORK   SYDNEY

HARD NUTS
of HISTORY

A & C BLACK
AN IMPRINT OF BLOOMSBURY
LONDON   NEW DELHI   NEW YORK   SYDNEY

TIMUR

HARD NUT
RATING: 9.3

HARDOMETER

CUNNING: 9
COURAGE: 9
SURVIVAL SKILLS: 9
RUTHLESSNESS: 10

KING NARMER

HARD NUT
RATING: 8.8

HARDOMETER

CUNNING: 9
COURAGE: 9
SURVIVAL SKILLS: 8
RUTHLESSNESS: 9

THUGINE

HARDOMETER

CUNNING: 8
COURAGE: 8
SURVIVAL SKILLS: 9
RUTHLESSNESS: 8

HARD NUT
RATING: 8.3

NEIL ARMSTRONG

HARD NUT
RATING: 8.5

HARDOMETER

CUNNING: 8
COURAGE: 10
SURVIVAL SKILLS: 9
RUTHLESSNESS: 7

HARD NUTS
of HISTORY

A & C BLACK
AN IMPRINT OF BLOOMSBURY
LONDON   NEW DELHI   NEW YORK   SYDNEY

HARD NUTS
of HISTORY

A & C BLACK
AN IMPRINT OF BLOOMSBURY
LONDON   NEW DELHI   NEW YORK   SYDNEY

HARD NUTS
of HISTORY

A & C BLACK
AN IMPRINT OF BLOOMSBURY
LONDON   NEW DELHI   NEW YORK   SYDNEY

HARD NUTS
of HISTORY

A & C BLACK
AN IMPRINT OF BLOOMSBURY
LONDON   NEW DELHI   NEW YORK   SYDNEY

HARD NUT RATING: 9

HARDOMETER

CUNNING: 9
COURAGE: 10
SURVIVAL SKILLS: 8
RUTHLESSNESS: 9

PELOPIDAS

ZENOBIA

HARD NUT RATING: 8.8

HARDOMETER

CUNNING: 9
COURAGE: 9
SURVIVAL SKILLS: 9
RUTHLESSNESS: 8

HARD NUT RATING: 9

HARDOMETER

CUNNING: 9
COURAGE: 9
SURVIVAL SKILLS: 10
RUTHLESSNESS: 8

RAMESSES THE GREAT

ATTILA THE HUN

HARDOMETER

CUNNING: 9
COURAGE: 8
SURVIVAL SKILLS: 9
RUTHLESSNESS: 10

HARD NUT RATING: 9

HARD NUTS
of HISTORY

A & C BLACK
AN IMPRINT OF BLOOMSBURY
LONDON   NEW DELHI   NEW YORK   SYDNEY

HARD NUTS
of HISTORY

A & C BLACK
AN IMPRINT OF BLOOMSBURY
LONDON   NEW DELHI   NEW YORK   SYDNEY

HARD NUTS
of HISTORY

A & C BLACK
AN IMPRINT OF BLOOMSBURY
LONDON   NEW DELHI   NEW YORK   SYDNEY

HARD NUTS
of HISTORY

A & C BLACK
AN IMPRINT OF BLOOMSBURY
LONDON   NEW DELHI   NEW YORK   SYDNEY

MARY KINGSLEY

HARDOMETER

CUNNING: 5
COURAGE: 9
SURVIVAL SKILLS: 8
RUTHLESSNESS: 5

HARD NUT RATING: 6.8

RE

HARD NUT RATING: 6.5

HARDOMETER

CUNNING: 5
COURAGE: 7
SURVIVAL SKILLS: 10
RUTHLESSNESS: 4

MURAD IV

HARD NUT RATING: 7.8

HARDOMETER

CUNNING: 8
COURAGE: 8
SURVIVAL SKILLS: 6
RUTHLESSNESS: 9

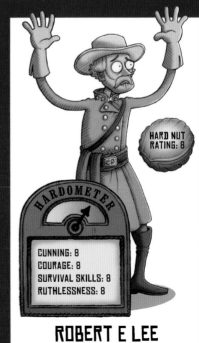

HARD NUT RATING: 8

HARDOMETER

CUNNING: 8
COURAGE: 8
SURVIVAL SKILLS: 8
RUTHLESSNESS: 8

ROBERT E LEE

HARD NUTS
OF HISTORY

A & C BLACK
AN IMPRINT OF BLOOMSBURY
LONDON   NEW DELHI   NEW YORK   SYDNEY

HARD NUTS
OF HISTORY

A & C BLACK
AN IMPRINT OF BLOOMSBURY
LONDON   NEW DELHI   NEW YORK   SYDNEY

HARD NUTS
OF HISTORY

A & C BLACK
AN IMPRINT OF BLOOMSBURY
LONDON   NEW DELHI   NEW YORK   SYDNEY

HARD NUTS
OF HISTORY

A & C BLACK
AN IMPRINT OF BLOOMSBURY
LONDON   NEW DELHI   NEW YORK   SYDNEY

CHE GUEVARA

HARD NUT RATING: 7.8

HARDOMETER

CUNNING: 7
COURAGE: 7
SURVIVAL SKILLS: 8
RUTHLESSNESS: 9

HARD NUT RATING: 7.3

HARDOMETER

CUNNING: 7
COURAGE: 7
SURVIVAL SKILLS: 8
RUTHLESSNESS: 7

ELIZABETH I

EMPEROR HADRIAN

HARD NUT RATING: 8.5

HARDOMETER

CUNNING: 8
COURAGE: 8
SURVIVAL SKILLS: 9
RUTHLESSNESS: 9

HIPPOCRATES

HARD NUT RATING: 6.3

HARDOMETER

CUNNING: 4
COURAGE: 9
SURVIVAL SKILLS: 8
RUTHLESSNESS: 4

HARD NUTS
of HISTORY

A & C BLACK
AN IMPRINT OF BLOOMSBURY
LONDON   NEW DELHI   NEW YORK   SYDNEY

HARD NUTS
of HISTORY

A & C BLACK
AN IMPRINT OF BLOOMSBURY
LONDON   NEW DELHI   NEW YORK   SYDNEY

HARD NUTS
of HISTORY

A & C BLACK
AN IMPRINT OF BLOOMSBURY
LONDON   NEW DELHI   NEW YORK   SYDNEY

HARD NUTS
of HISTORY

A & C BLACK
AN IMPRINT OF BLOOMSBURY
LONDON   NEW DELHI   NEW YORK   SYDNEY

THE TRUNG SISTERS

HARD NUT RATING: 7.8

HARDOMETER
CUNNING: 8
COURAGE: 9
SURVIVAL SKILLS: 6
RUTHLESSNESS: 8

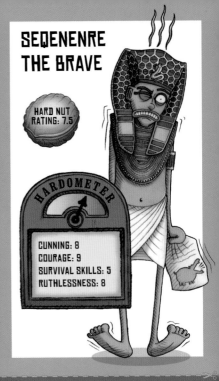

SEQENENRE THE BRAVE

HARD NUT RATING: 7.5

HARDOMETER
CUNNING: 8
COURAGE: 9
SURVIVAL SKILLS: 5
RUTHLESSNESS: 8

ROBIN HOOD

HARD NUT RATING: 8

HARDOMETER
CUNNING: 8
COURAGE: 9
SURVIVAL SKILLS: 8
RUTHLESSNESS: 7

SCOTT OF THE ANTARCTIC

HARD NUT RATING: 7

HARDOMETER
CUNNING: 5
COURAGE: 9
SURVIVAL SKILLS: 8
RUTHLESSNESS: 6

HARD NUTS
of HISTORY

A & C BLACK
AN IMPRINT OF BLOOMSBURY
LONDON NEW DELHI NEW YORK SYDNEY

HARD NUTS
of HISTORY

A & C BLACK
AN IMPRINT OF BLOOMSBURY
LONDON NEW DELHI NEW YORK SYDNEY

HARD NUTS
of HISTORY

A & C BLACK
AN IMPRINT OF BLOOMSBURY
LONDON NEW DELHI NEW YORK SYDNEY

HARD NUTS
of HISTORY

A & C BLACK
AN IMPRINT OF BLOOMSBURY
LONDON NEW DELHI NEW YORK SYDNEY

PISISTRATUS

HARD NUT RATING: 8.5

HARDOMETER

CUNNING: 9
COURAGE: 8
SURVIVAL SKILLS: 9
RUTHLESSNESS: 8

SULLA

HARD NUT RATING: 10

PROSCRIPTIONS

HARDOMETER

CUNNING: 10
COURAGE: 10
SURVIVAL SKILLS: 10
RUTHLESSNESS: 10

HARD NUT RATING: 8.8

HARDOMETER

CUNNING: 9
COURAGE: 9
SURVIVAL SKILLS: 9
RUTHLESSNESS: 8

PTOLEMY I

MAHMUD OF GHAZNI

HARD NUT RATING: 8

HARDOMETER

CUNNING: 7
COURAGE: 8
SURVIVAL SKILLS: 8
RUTHLESSNESS: 9

HARD NUTS
of HISTORY

A & C BLACK
AN IMPRINT OF BLOOMSBURY
LONDON   NEW DELHI   NEW YORK   SYDNEY

HARD NUTS
of HISTORY

A & C BLACK
AN IMPRINT OF BLOOMSBURY
LONDON   NEW DELHI   NEW YORK   SYDNEY

HARD NUTS
of HISTORY

A & C BLACK
AN IMPRINT OF BLOOMSBURY
LONDON   NEW DELHI   NEW YORK   SYDNEY

HARD NUTS
of HISTORY

A & C BLACK
AN IMPRINT OF BLOOMSBURY
LONDON   NEW DELHI   NEW YORK   SYDNEY

SIR WALTER RALEIGH

HARD NUT RATING: 7

HARDOMETER

CUNNING: 6
COURAGE: 8
SURVIVAL SKILLS: 7
RUTHLESSNESS: 7

THESEUS

HARD NUT RATING: 8

HARDOMETER

CUNNING: 7
COURAGE: 10
SURVIVAL SKILLS: 6
RUTHLESSNESS: 9

SULEIMAN THE MAGNIFICENT

HARD NUT RATING: 7

HARDOMETER

CUNNING: 7
COURAGE: 7
SURVIVAL SKILLS: 8
RUTHLESSNESS: 6

HARD NUT RATING: 9

HARDOMETER

CUNNING: 9
COURAGE: 10
SURVIVAL SKILLS: 8
RUTHLESSNESS: 9

VIOLETTE SZABO

HARD NUTS
of HISTORY

A & C BLACK
AN IMPRINT OF BLOOMSBURY
LONDON   NEW DELHI   NEW YORK   SYDNEY

HARD NUTS
of HISTORY

A & C BLACK
AN IMPRINT OF BLOOMSBURY
LONDON   NEW DELHI   NEW YORK   SYDNEY

HARD NUTS
of HISTORY

A & C BLACK
AN IMPRINT OF BLOOMSBURY
LONDON   NEW DELHI   NEW YORK   SYDNEY

HARD NUTS
of HISTORY

A & C BLACK
AN IMPRINT OF BLOOMSBURY
LONDON   NEW DELHI   NEW YORK   SYDNEY

ASHOKA THE GREAT

HARD NUT RATING: 6.3

HARDOMETER

CUNNING: 7
COURAGE: 8
SURVIVAL SKILLS: 5
RUTHLESSNESS: 5

WU ZETIAN

HARD NUT RATING: 8.5

HARDOMETER

CUNNING: 8
COURAGE: 8
SURVIVAL SKILLS: 9
RUTHLESSNESS: 9

FLAVIUS BELISARIUS

HARD NUT RATING: 9

HARDOMETER

CUNNING: 9
COURAGE: 9
SURVIVAL SKILLS: 9
RUTHLESSNESS: 9

CLEON

HARD NUT RATING: 8

WANTED

HARDOMETER

CUNNING: 7
COURAGE: 9
SURVIVAL SKILLS: 6
RUTHLESSNESS: 10

HARD NUTS
of HISTORY

A & C BLACK
AN IMPRINT OF BLOOMSBURY
LONDON   NEW DELHI   NEW YORK   SYDNEY

HARD NUTS
of HISTORY

A & C BLACK
AN IMPRINT OF BLOOMSBURY
LONDON   NEW DELHI   NEW YORK   SYDNEY

HARD NUTS
of HISTORY

A & C BLACK
AN IMPRINT OF BLOOMSBURY
LONDON   NEW DELHI   NEW YORK   SYDNEY

HARD NUTS
of HISTORY

A & C BLACK
AN IMPRINT OF BLOOMSBURY
LONDON   NEW DELHI   NEW YORK   SYDNEY

HONGWU

HARD NUT RATING: 9

HARDOMETER

CUNNING: 9
COURAGE: 9
SURVIVAL SKILLS: 9
RUTHLESSNESS: 9

ESARHADDON

HARD NUT RATING: 8.5

HARDOMETER

CUNNING: 8
COURAGE: 9
SURVIVAL SKILLS: 8
RUTHLESSNESS: 9

SIR GAWAIN

HARD NUT RATING: 7.8

HARDOMETER

CUNNING: 7
COURAGE: 9
SURVIVAL SKILLS: 7
RUTHLESSNESS: 8

PONCE DE LEON

HARD NUT RATING: 9

HARDOMETER

CUNNING: 9
COURAGE: 9
SURVIVAL SKILLS: 8
RUTHLESSNESS: 10

HARD NUTS
OF HISTORY

A & C BLACK
AN IMPRINT OF BLOOMSBURY
LONDON   NEW DELHI   NEW YORK   SYDNEY

HARD NUTS
OF HISTORY

A & C BLACK
AN IMPRINT OF BLOOMSBURY
LONDON   NEW DELHI   NEW YORK   SYDNEY

HARD NUTS
OF HISTORY

A & C BLACK
AN IMPRINT OF BLOOMSBURY
LONDON   NEW DELHI   NEW YORK   SYDNEY

HARD NUTS
OF HISTORY

A & C BLACK
AN IMPRINT OF BLOOMSBURY
LONDON   NEW DELHI   NEW YORK   SYDNEY

LYSANDER

NAVARCH
DEPUTY ADMIRAL

HARD NUT
RATING: 8.5

HARDOMETER

CUNNING: 9
COURAGE: 8
SURVIVAL SKILLS: 9
RUTHLESSNESS: 8

TARQUIN THE PROUD

HARD NUT
RATING: 8.3

HARDOMETER

CUNNING: 8
COURAGE: 7
SURVIVAL SKILLS: 9
RUTHLESSNESS: 9

MENTUHOTEP II

HARD NUT
RATING: 8.5

FIGHTING
TO DO

HARDOMETER

CUNNING: 8
COURAGE: 9
SURVIVAL SKILLS: 8
RUTHLESSNESS: 9

NAPOLEON

HARD NUT
RATING: 8

HARDOMETER

CUNNING: 8
COURAGE: 8
SURVIVAL SKILLS: 8
RUTHLESSNESS: 8

HARD NUTS
of HISTORY

A & C BLACK
AN IMPRINT OF BLOOMSBURY
LONDON   NEW DELHI   NEW YORK   SYDNEY

HARD NUTS
of HISTORY

A & C BLACK
AN IMPRINT OF BLOOMSBURY
LONDON   NEW DELHI   NEW YORK   SYDNEY

HARD NUTS
of HISTORY

A & C BLACK
AN IMPRINT OF BLOOMSBURY
LONDON   NEW DELHI   NEW YORK   SYDNEY

HARD NUTS
of HISTORY

A & C BLACK
AN IMPRINT OF BLOOMSBURY
LONDON   NEW DELHI   NEW YORK   SYDNEY

VASCO DA GAMA

HARD NUT RATING: 9

HARDOMETER

CUNNING: 9
COURAGE: 9
SURVIVAL SKILLS: 9
RUTHLESSNESS: 9

ANANSI

HARD NUT RATING: 7.5

HARDOMETER

CUNNING: 10
COURAGE: 5
SURVIVAL SKILLS: 5
RUTHLESSNESS: 10

QUEEN TAMAR OF GEORGIA

HARD NUT RATING: 7

HARDOMETER

CUNNING: 8
COURAGE: 8
SURVIVAL SKILLS: 6
RUTHLESSNESS: 6

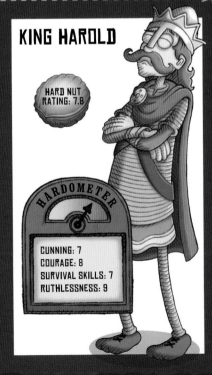

KING HAROLD

HARD NUT RATING: 7.8

HARDOMETER

CUNNING: 7
COURAGE: 8
SURVIVAL SKILLS: 7
RUTHLESSNESS: 9

HARD NUTS
of HISTORY

A & C BLACK
AN IMPRINT OF BLOOMSBURY
LONDON   NEW DELHI   NEW YORK   SYDNEY

HARD NUTS
of HISTORY

A & C BLACK
AN IMPRINT OF BLOOMSBURY
LONDON   NEW DELHI   NEW YORK   SYDNEY

HARD NUTS
of HISTORY

A & C BLACK
AN IMPRINT OF BLOOMSBURY
LONDON   NEW DELHI   NEW YORK   SYDNEY

HARD NUTS
of HISTORY

A & C BLACK
AN IMPRINT OF BLOOMSBURY
LONDON   NEW DELHI   NEW YORK   SYDNEY

KING CETSHWAYO

HARD NUT RATING: 8.5

HARDOMETER

CUNNING: 9
COURAGE: 9
SURVIVAL SKILLS: 7
RUTHLESSNESS: 9

QUEEN ARTEMISIA OF HALICARNASSUS

HARD NUT RATING: 8.3

HARDOMETER

CUNNING: 8
COURAGE: 9
SURVIVAL SKILLS: 8
RUTHLESSNESS: 8

VERCINGETORIX

HARD NUT RATING: 7.5

HARDOMETER

CUNNING: 7
COURAGE: 8
SURVIVAL SKILLS: 7
RUTHLESSNESS: 8

THEMISTOCLES

HARD NUT RATING: 8.5

HARDOMETER

CUNNING: 9
COURAGE: 9
SURVIVAL SKILLS: 7
RUTHLESSNESS: 9

HARD NUTS of HISTORY

A & C BLACK
AN IMPRINT OF BLOOMSBURY
LONDON NEW DELHI NEW YORK SYDNEY

HARD NUTS of HISTORY

A & C BLACK
AN IMPRINT OF BLOOMSBURY
LONDON NEW DELHI NEW YORK SYDNEY

HARD NUTS of HISTORY

A & C BLACK
AN IMPRINT OF BLOOMSBURY
LONDON NEW DELHI NEW YORK SYDNEY

HARD NUTS of HISTORY

A & C BLACK
AN IMPRINT OF BLOOMSBURY
LONDON NEW DELHI NEW YORK SYDNEY

CYRUS THE GREAT

CONQUERING LIST

HARD NUT RATING: 8.3

HARDOMETER

CUNNING: 9
COURAGE: 9
SURVIVAL SKILLS: 6
RUTHLESSNESS: 9

HARD NUT RATING: 8

HARDOMETER

CUNNING: 8
COURAGE: 9
SURVIVAL SKILLS: 7
RUTHLESSNESS: 8

CAMBYSES II

HARD NUT RATING: 5

HARDOMETER

CUNNING: 6
COURAGE: 7
SURVIVAL SKILLS: 5
RUTHLESSNESS: 2

QUETZALCOATL

BURKE AND WILLS

HARDOMETER

CUNNING: 5
COURAGE: 8
SURVIVAL SKILLS: 4
RUTHLESSNESS: 8

HARD NUT RATING: 6.3

HARD NUTS of HISTORY

A & C BLACK
AN IMPRINT OF BLOOMSBURY

LONDON   NEW DELHI   NEW YORK   SYDNEY

HARD NUTS of HISTORY

A & C BLACK
AN IMPRINT OF BLOOMSBURY

LONDON   NEW DELHI   NEW YORK   SYDNEY

HARD NUTS of HISTORY

A & C BLACK
AN IMPRINT OF BLOOMSBURY

LONDON   NEW DELHI   NEW YORK   SYDNEY

HARD NUTS of HISTORY

A & C BLACK
AN IMPRINT OF BLOOMSBURY

LONDON   NEW DELHI   NEW YORK   SYDNEY

ALCIBIADES

HARD NUT RATING: 7.8

HARDOMETER

CUNNING: 9
COURAGE: 5
SURVIVAL SKILLS: 8
RUTHLESSNESS: 9

CARACTACUS

HARD NUT RATING: 8.8

HARDOMETER

CUNNING: 8
COURAGE: 9
SURVIVAL SKILLS: 10
RUTHLESSNESS: 8

AHMOSE I

HARD NUT RATING: 8.8

HARDOMETER

CUNNING: 8
COURAGE: 9
SURVIVAL SKILLS: 9
RUTHLESSNESS: 9

BOUDICA

HARD NUT RATING: 7.5

HARDOMETER

CUNNING: 7
COURAGE: 9
SURVIVAL SKILLS: 7
RUTHLESSNESS: 7

HARD NUTS
OF HISTORY

A & C BLACK
AN IMPRINT OF BLOOMSBURY
LONDON   NEW DELHI   NEW YORK   SYDNEY

HARD NUTS
OF HISTORY

A & C BLACK
AN IMPRINT OF BLOOMSBURY
LONDON   NEW DELHI   NEW YORK   SYDNEY

HARD NUTS
OF HISTORY

A & C BLACK
AN IMPRINT OF BLOOMSBURY
LONDON   NEW DELHI   NEW YORK   SYDNEY

HARD NUTS
OF HISTORY

A & C BLACK
AN IMPRINT OF BLOOMSBURY
LONDON   NEW DELHI   NEW YORK   SYDNEY

DAVID LIVINGSTONE

HARD NUT
RATING: 7.5

HARDOMETER

CUNNING: 6
COURAGE: 10
SURVIVAL SKILLS: 9
RUTHLESSNESS: 5

FUMO LIYONGO

HARD NUT
RATING: 6.5

HARDOMETER

CUNNING: 9
COURAGE: 7
SURVIVAL SKILLS: 5
RUTHLESSNESS: 5

HARD NUT
RATING: 8

HARDOMETER

CUNNING: 8
COURAGE: 6
SURVIVAL SKILLS: 8
RUTHLESSNESS: 10

ASHURNASIRPAL II

SIEGFRIED SASSOON

HARD NUT
RATING: 7.5

HARDOMETER

CUNNING: 7
COURAGE: 9
SURVIVAL SKILLS: 7
RUTHLESSNESS: 7

HARD NUTS
of HISTORY

A & C BLACK
AN IMPRINT OF BLOOMSBURY
LONDON NEW DELHI NEW YORK SYDNEY

HARD NUTS
of HISTORY

A & C BLACK
AN IMPRINT OF BLOOMSBURY
LONDON NEW DELHI NEW YORK SYDNEY

HARD NUTS
of HISTORY

A & C BLACK
AN IMPRINT OF BLOOMSBURY
LONDON NEW DELHI NEW YORK SYDNEY

HARD NUTS
of HISTORY

A & C BLACK
AN IMPRINT OF BLOOMSBURY
LONDON NEW DELHI NEW YORK SYDNEY